Called to Listen

FORTY DAYS OF DEVOTION

Michelle J. Goff

Iron Rose Sister Ministries

Michelle J. Goff / CreateSpace
Iron Rose Sister Ministries
www.IronRoseSister.com
1-501-593-4849

Book Layout ©2013 BookDesignTemplates.com

Because of the dynamic nature of the Internet, any web addresses or links contained in this book may have changed since publication and may no longer be valid. The views expressed in this work are solely those of the author and do not necessarily reflect the views of the publisher, and the publisher hereby disclaims any responsibility for them.

Called to Listen / Michelle J. Goff.—1st ed.
ISBN 978-0-9963602-8-9 (sc)

Contents

Acknowledgements...i

Preface by Dr. Bill Richardson.. 1

Introduction to Listening..3

Introductory Lesson in Small Group Context 5

Week 1: *Listening to the Good Shepherd*.........................7

    Week 1: Weekly Reflections 25

Week 2: *Listening to the Creator*.....................................29

    Week 2: Weekly Reflections 47

Week 3: *Listening to the Father*.......................................51

    Week 3: Weekly Reflections 71

Week 4: *Listening to the Son*..75

    Week 4: Weekly Reflections 93

Week 5: *Listening to the Spirit*...97

    Week 5: Weekly Reflections 113

Week 6: *Listening through the Five Senses*...........117

    Week 6: Weekly Reflections 131

Conclusion:..135

Appendix A: Iron Rose Sister Ministries Bible Study Format 137

Appendix B: Guide for the Facilitator 141

About the Author...143

About Iron Rose Sister Ministries 147

To those who listen and strive to hear.

Acknowledgements

Listening is a challenge for me. Yet God always hears me when I call and has been patient in my process of learning how to better listen to Him. My eternal thanks and may all the glory be to the One who listens.

Special thanks to my parents, who can't wait to hear the God stories from my trips and never tire of listening to me talk—no matter what the topic. The give and take of our listening has been a foundational example in my relationships with others.

And to my sisters who have listened to me as the "bossy sister" growing up, even talking in other languages through my dreams. You will always be among those I want to listen to.

Thanks to Katie Forbess, IRSM Board President, who never hesitates to say what needs to be said, even if I would rather not hear it. I thank you for being God's vessel in my life. May we never cease to dream of all God can and will do through us and through this ministry!

And a big thank you to the Tuesday night pilot study of this book in English. Jocelynn, Erica, Carolyn, Carol, Emily, Haley, Kayla, and Samantha, your listening and sharing were instrumental in equipping others to listen.

Since this book is being released in conjunction with the second IRSM Destination Retreat, *Called to Listen*, I wish to express my appreciation for the team of women who are using their talents to facilitate an excellent listening experience and equipping event for women from across the country: Tatiane Borba, Carol Busselle, Katie Forbess, Carole Gastineau, Jocelynn Goff, Wendy Neill, Erica Peck, Terri Rine, Débora Rodrigo, Susan Shirel, Mandy Jo Steil, Carla Sumner, Michelle Supratman. Thank you!

To the proofers, I thank you for your tireless effort and unique talents: Christa Duve, Carla Sumner, and Mackenzie Lancaster (among other intern responsibilities).

And to Sherry Hubright, who helped facilitate a writing retreat in preparation and study for this book, thanks for listening.

Huge thanks to the following specific individuals for the use of their talents:

➢ Kenneth Mills for the cover design.
➢ Geoffrey Wyatt for the bio picture.
➢ Joel Friedlander, Book Template Designs.

Preface by Dr. Bill Richardson

O ur world is filled with noise, distractions, and frenetic activity. Over the din of our daily existence God's Word admonishes: "Be still and know that I am God" (Psalm 46:10). Being still is no small challenge! The clamor of our lives is so pervasive that we have been conditioned to avoid silence and solitude. We find ourselves home alone and we search for the TV remote. We pull out of the drive-way each morning for our commute to work and reach for the radio. Could it be that we beat back the silence with the racket of the world because silence leaves us alone ... with God!? This noisy environment is so different than what David experienced as he tended his father's sheep in the fields surrounding Bethlehem. Keeping watch over defenseless animals, David slept under a canopy of stars and reflected on the mean-ing of life and God's plan for man (Ps. 8). Providing for the needs of the flock, David grew in his appreciation for God's care for him (Ps. 23). The natural response to all of this "alone time" was David's worship through prayers accompanied by music. David's first psalms were his reply to all he had "heard" from God in the creation that surrounded him (Ps. 19). He chose to fill his silence with praise. In this way, David's relationship with God was nurtured. It was a relationship that would ultimately sustain him when his own life became one of frenetic activity and he was chal-lenged with the distractions of sin and loss. As God's people, we cannot survive the "noise" without alone time in communion with God.

You hold in your hands a book that is designed to instruct you in the discipline of listening. It provides forty days of timely guidance to devel-oping the "ears to hear" God's Word. Following his baptism in the Jordan River, Jesus was led into a wilderness of solitude for forty days. This time of fasting and communion with the Father strengthened him to face the Tempter. These crucial forty days launched Jesus into a ministry marked by self-denial and dependence on God's Spirit, culminating at the cross. He calls you, His disciple, to follow in His footsteps. Living like Jesus in the 21st Century is "Mission Impossible," if we refuse the solitude and quietness necessary to listen to His voice. Communication is the "oxygen" of any relationship and real communication depends heavily on active listening. Nothing is more vital to our lives than to communicate frequently and meaningfully with the very Source of Life!

Michelle Goff has dedicated her efforts, in an ever-expanding ministry, to providing tools and training for Christian living to her sisters in Christ. I applaud her for recognizing the vital need in every disciple's life to listen to the Master's voice and for providing yet another wonderful resource. I am personally unaware of any other practical guide to this critical topic. Michelle has provided thoughtful introductions drawn from her wide experience as a missionary to provide a meaningful context to key biblical texts which have been carefully selected and organized. "Listening" exercises and questions which are designed to provoke careful reflection follow. The approach taken will involve you both in solitude and in communion with fellow disciples. I believe the next forty days will be a time of transformation in your life if you will devote the time necessary to read, meditate, and complete these exercises. I encourage you to accept this book of devotions as your personal invitation to take a daily break from the noise of your life in order to "Be still and know that God is God!"

Introduction to Listening

How do we fulfill the commands in Matthew 22:34-39 to *love God? And to love others? Listen to God. Listen to others.*

Our Heavenly Father has a message that we have each been called to hear, but are you listening? Amid the noisy world we live in, listening has become a lost art. We know that "anyone with ears to hear should listen and understand" (NLT). But how should we listen? What is God saying?

We may not hear from a burning bush like Moses, but we *can* hear His voice through His Word, through nature, through Christian brothers and sisters, even through silence... But again, the question we must ask ourselves is, "Are we listening?"

Devotion to God is a high priority for listening. When we are devoted to Him, we give Him our attention—full and undivided. Devotion implies dedication, admiration, and time—all elements needed as we engage in deeper relationship with our Father and fulfill our calling to listen.

Through these 40 days of devotion, we will explore and experience listening to God, and to others, in a variety of ways.

Each week will present a different focus for our listening exercises. Some days' activities will resonate deep within your soul, issuing echoes of God's voice. Other practices of listening may fall on deaf ears. No matter what your reaction or your initial impression, I encourage you to keep listening.

Each day brings an opportunity to open our heart, soul, mind, and strength to what we need to hear. You will be encouraged, challenged, blessed, and even tested. Keep listening.

God has so much He wants to tell us, so much to share, guide, and remind. Are you listening?

Week 1: *Listening to the Good Shepherd*

Week 2: *Listening to the Creator*

Week 3: *Listening to the Father*

Week 4: *Listening to the Son*

Week 5: *Listening to the Holy Spirit*

Week 6: *Listening through the five senses*

There will be *Daily Listening Exercises* to be done individually. We call them exercises because they stretch our spiritual muscles and train us in the discipline of listening.

Weekly Reflections will be shared in the context of community, with your Iron Rose Sisters (Christian sisters that serve as iron sharpening iron, encouraging and inspiring one another to be as beautiful as a rose, in spite of a few thorns).

Thank you for joining us the devotion to listening.

Small Group Kickoff, Starting Week 1

G o around the room and have each woman share:
- Her name,
- What kind of music she likes to listen to, and
- What kind of music she does *not* like to listen to.

How does the music you like make you feel?

How do you feel when you listen to the music you don't like?

How do you feel when you have heard God's voice?

Are some of the descriptions of how you feel the same—listening to music you like and listening to God's voice?

Is listening to God's voice always pleasant? Why or why not?

How do we hear God's voice?

Throughout the next 40 days, we will learn and practice a variety of ways to listen to God. The *Daily Exercises* will introduce us to an assortment of methods for listening.

We can also refer to them as *Listening Practices*—none of us have them perfected, but we need to train ourselves to listen. And it takes practice. If you don't feel like you listen well one day, don't get discouraged. Start again tomorrow and listen as best as you can. With practice, you will get better and you will begin to hear God's voice more clearly.

Gathering together for *Weekly Reflections* will allow us to rejoice in what we have heard and encourage one another to keep listening.

Note for the Facilitator: Feel free to go over and highlight some of the days in each week when you gather with your small group of Iron Rose Sisters. Additional suggestions and directions are included in the Facilitator's Guide (pg. 141-142).

Week 1, Day 1
Knowing the Voice
of the Good Shepherd

Sheep are dumb. But there is one thing that makes them smarter than many of us: They know the voice of the Good Shepherd.

Read John 10:1-18 and reflect on the questions that follow as we listen to the Good Shepherd's voice today. (The NLT version is included below, but feel free to read it in multiple versions to hear the Good Shepherd's voice in different and new ways.)

10 "I tell you the truth, anyone who sneaks over the wall of a sheepfold, rather than going through the gate, must surely be a thief and a robber! ² But the one who enters through the gate is the shepherd of the sheep. ³ The gatekeeper opens the gate for him, and the sheep recognize his voice and come to him. He calls his own sheep by name and leads them out. ⁴ After he has gathered his own flock, he walks ahead of them, and they follow him because they know his voice. ⁵ They won't follow a stranger; they will run from him because they don't know his voice."

⁶ Those who heard Jesus use this illustration didn't understand what he meant, ⁷ so he explained it to them: "I tell you the truth, I am the gate for the sheep. ⁸ All who came before me were thieves and robbers. But the true sheep did not listen to them. ⁹ Yes, I am the gate. Those who come in through me will be saved. They will

come and go freely and will find good pastures. [10] The thief's purpose is to steal and kill and destroy. My purpose is to give them a rich and satisfying life.

[11] "I am the good shepherd. The good shepherd sacrifices his life for the sheep. [12] A hired hand will run when he sees a wolf coming. He will abandon the sheep because they don't belong to him and he isn't their shepherd. And so the wolf attacks them and scatters the flock. [13] The hired hand runs away because he's working only for the money and doesn't really care about the sheep.

[14] "I am the good shepherd; I know my own sheep, and they know me, [15] just as my Father knows me and I know the Father. So I sacrifice my life for the sheep. [16] I have other sheep, too, that are not in this sheepfold. I must bring them also. They will listen to my voice, and there will be one flock with one shepherd.

[17] "The Father loves me because I sacrifice my life so I may take it back again. [18] No one can take my life from me. I sacrifice it voluntarily. For I have the authority to lay it down when I want to and also to take it up again. For this is what my Father has commanded."

What does the Good Shepherd's voice sound like?

What kind of things does He say?

What makes the sheep trust His voice?

Why do they trust His voice over any stranger's voice?

When was the first time the sheep recognized the shepherd's voice?

How do you think the sheep felt when carried by the Good Shepherd after getting injured or wandering too far?

How is the voice of the Good Shepherd speaking to you today?

Week 1, Day 2
What the Good Shepherd Wants to Say

Yesterday, we introduced the importance of knowing the voice of the Good Shepherd. But how can we hear His voice? And even if we hear it, are we listening?

Psalm 23 illustrates the heart of the Good Shepherd as comforter, guide, protector, and provider.

Read Psalm 23 (ESV) below and underline the portions of this psalm that most speak to your heart today. Read it more than one time and in more than one version.

There are several songs written directly from this psalm. Find a songbook, a YouTube® video or another way to listen to and sing along with a song from this psalm today.

We are listening carefully to the voice of the Good Shepherd through scripture and through song. And may His words of comfort go with you throughout your day.

23 The LORD is my shepherd; I shall not want.
² He makes me lie down in green pastures.
He leads me beside still waters.
³ He restores my soul.
He leads me in paths of righteousness
 for his name's sake.
⁴Even though I walk through the valley of the shadow of death,
 I will fear no evil,
for you are with me;
 your rod and your staff,
 they comfort me.

⁵You prepare a table before me
  in the presence of my enemies;
you anoint my head with oil;
  my cup overflows.
⁶Surely goodness and mercy shall follow me
  all the days of my life,
and I shall dwell in the house of the LORD
  forever.

Notes, drawings, or thoughts from listening to the Good Shepherd today:

Week 1, Day 3
Listen patiently
(especially when you don't understand)

I'm waiting… but how long am I supposed to wait?

I'm listening… but I'm not sure that I'm hearing anything.

I'm waiting… but this is not what I wanted to hear.

I'm listening… but I'm not sure I get it, or that I want to.

Habakkuk 2:3 (ESV)

**³ For still the vision awaits its appointed time;
it hastens to the end—it will not lie.
If it seems slow, wait for it;
it will surely come; it will not delay.**

Isaiah 55:8-9 (ESV)

**⁸ For my thoughts are not your thoughts,
neither are your ways my ways, declares the LORD.
⁹ For as the heavens are higher than the earth,
so are my ways higher than your ways
and my thoughts than your thoughts.**

Even when the Good Shepherd tells you **where** to go, **what** to do, **how** to live, or **who** to follow, you may not understand the **why**.

Yet, when I'm honest with myself, I'm glad that I don't always understand the why. Because it means that God is God and I am not. He has the ultimate perspective. I am a lowly sheep in need of a Good Shepherd.

As my Good Shepherd, He knows when a lion is lurking around the corner. And while I may get frustrated to be deterred from my current path, I must trust that He sees the big picture. Everything He does is out of love—for my own protection and wellbeing.

Sometimes we listen best through the experiences of others or reminders of times when the Good Shepherd has been faithful in the past.

Describe a time in which the Good Shepherd blessed, protected, or provided for you—a story of something that you didn't understand at the time, but later recognized the hand of the Good Shepherd guiding you in His wisdom.

Additional notes, drawings, or thoughts from listening to the Good Shepherd today:

Week 1, Day 4
Listen and Walk in His Ways

The Good Shepherd is a guide for the sheep. We sheep cannot find pasture or still waters on our own. And when we try to find our own path or make our own way, we get into trouble and sadden God.

Psalm 81:13 (ESV)

Oh, that my people would listen to me,
that Israel would walk in my ways!

God often laments that His sheep do not listen or walk in His ways. We tend to want to do things on our own. We are stubborn. And even if we started out listening, we try to change God's message to fit our own agenda, like Balaam.

And when we refuse to listen, we become blind, again like Balaam.

Sheep. Donkeys. God will use any animal or anything in our path to illustrate His point and remind us to listen. Because left to our own devices, desires, and design, we are asking for trouble and headed toward destruction.

It really is wisest to listen to God the first time and to choose to walk in His ways.

In summary of the story, Balak, king of Moab, is fearful of the Israelites. He recognizes that they are a protected and numerous people. So, he sends the following message to Balaam, a prophet of God (Num. 22:5b-6, ESV).

5b "Behold, a people has come out of Egypt. They cover the face of the earth, and they are dwelling opposite me. 6 Come now, curse

this people for me, since they are too mighty for me. Perhaps I shall be able to defeat them and drive them from the land, for I know that he whom you bless is blessed, and he whom you curse is cursed."

Balaam hears the message and consults with God (after God initiates the conversation, Num. 22:12-13, ESV).

¹² God said to Balaam, "You shall not go with them. You shall not curse the people, for they are blessed." ¹³ So Balaam rose in the morning and said to the princes of Balak, "Go to your own land, for the LORD has refused to let me go with you."

Did Balaam listen to what God said?

Did Balaam change the message? How so or how not?

Read Numbers 22—24. It may appear to be a long passage, but the narrative of this story is rich with application for our listening to the Good Shepherd.

How did Balaam do with his listening?

How did Balak do with his listening?

What do we learn from this story and our listening practices?

What does it mean to listen to the voice of God—above all our own thoughts and desires?

Numbers 23:19 (ESV)

[19] God is not man, that he should lie,
   or a son of man, that he should change his mind.
Has he said, and will he not do it?
   Or has he spoken, and will he not fulfill it?

Additional notes, drawings, or thoughts from listening to the Good Shepherd today:

Week 1, Day 5
The Gate for the Sheep

The Good Shepherd has multiple roles He plays in the life of His sheep.

What does it mean that He is the gate for the sheep (John 10:7, 9)?

Let's reread that portion of John 10:7-10 (NIV).

⁷Therefore Jesus said again, "Very truly I tell you, I am the gate for the sheep. ⁸All who have come before me are thieves and robbers, but the sheep have not listened to them. ⁹I am the gate; whoever enters through me will be saved. They will come in and go out, and find pasture. ¹⁰The thief comes only to steal and kill and destroy; I have come that they may have life, and have it to the full.

An alternate translation for verse 9 is "…whoever enters through me will be kept safe…"

This secondary translation of Jesus as the gate for the sheep is not negating His role as our Savior, mediator, and way to God. John 14:6 and many other passages clearly state that we cannot gain access to the Father, nor enter the kingdom, without going through the Son. However, let's open wide our ears to listen and explore another illustration of Jesus as the gate for the sheep.

What is the purpose of a gate?

Who does it keep out?

Who does it keep in?

How is the Good Shepherd's desire to give us an abundant life enhanced by His description as the gate for the sheep?

Additional notes, drawings, or thoughts from listening to the Good Shepherd today:

Week 1, Day 6
The Great I AM's Words of Life

In John 10, we have seen two of the self-proclaimed I AM descriptions of Jesus: the Good Shepherd and the gate for the sheep. Today, we will listen to the other I AM descriptions of Jesus in the book of John.

- Read through each section of Scripture three times.
- Take a moment to reflect and meditate on each one.
- Draw something to the side of each of these verses as a reminder of that characteristic of Jesus, the Good Shepherd.
- Select one of the verses to write out on a notecard, or to set as a reminder on your phone.

John 6:35 (ESV)

³⁵ Jesus said to them, "I am the bread of life; whoever comes to me shall not hunger, and whoever believes in me shall never thirst.

John 8:12 (ESV)

¹² Again Jesus spoke to them, saying, "I am the light of the world. Whoever follows me will not walk in darkness, but will have the light of life."

John 11:25-26 (ESV)

²⁵ Jesus said to her, "I am the resurrection and the life. Whoever believes in me, though he die, yet shall he live, ²⁶ and everyone who lives and believes in me shall never die. Do you believe this?"

John 14:6 (ESV)

⁶ Jesus said to him, "I am the way, and the truth, and the life. No one comes to the Father except through me.

John 15:1, 5 (NIV)

¹ "I am the true vine, and my Father is the gardener."

⁵ "I am the vine; you are the branches. If you remain in me and I in you, you will bear much fruit; apart from me you can do nothing."

Which of these characteristic descriptions of the Good Shepherd do you most need to listen to today and why?

And what is the Good Shepherd telling you through that same vivid reminder of who He is? Feel free to write it out, draw it, or verbally share it with others.

Week 1, Day 7
Listening to the Voice of the Good Shepherd

"I AM THE GOOD SHEPHERD.
I KNOW MY SHEEP
AND MY SHEEP KNOW ME—"
JOHN 10:14

Take some time to meditate on this verse. You can color the picture or draw your own. Re-write the verse in your own hand-writing. Spend some time in the arms of the Good Shepherd, listening to His voice. Feel free to make notes on what you hear.

Week 1: **Listening to the Good Shepherd**

Each week, when we gather together, we will share the ways in which we have listened, what we have heard, and how we can continue to encourage and inspire one another in our listening. We have dedicated a time each day to listen to God and now we will devote some time listening to one another.

The following are the two questions we will ask and answer together each week.

1) What have you heard from the Good Shepherd this week?

2) Which day's listening activity most resonated with you? And why that one?

Now, based on what we have each heard, we will share in the Common Threads (an Iron Rose Sister Ministries way of making any lesson, teaching, or reflection very personal and practical). The Common Threads help us focus in on the specifics of what we have heard and guide us into putting those things into practice, all in the context of community. They also serve as a form of spiritual journaling, which is why I encourage you to date them and look back later to see your growth.

Each woman's answers will be different because we hear unique things and each face different spiritual battles at any given moment. However, we can encourage one another to grow and bloom in those areas, remove thorns that hinder that growth, and hold each other accountable as iron sharpening iron.

Common Threads:

Date _____

An area in which you'd like to grow or bloom.

_____

_____

A thorn you'd like to remove.

_____

_____

An area in which you'd like to dig deeper or need someone to hold you accountable. (How can we, as a group, help you continue to listen or put into practice what you have heard?)

_____

_____

A message of hope, an encouraging word, or scripture from your time of listening.

_____

_____

Close each week in a time of prayer thanking God for what you have heard and bringing to God the requests shared through the Common Threads. This is an opportunity to join as one voice in our struggles, to rejoice in our victories, and to continue to listen to God and one another.

Week 2, Day 1
The Heavens Declare...

Psalm 19:1 (ESV)

**The heavens declare the glory of God,
and the sky above proclaims his handiwork.**

The booming voice of a thunderstorm, the promise in a rainbow, the majesty in the mountains, the babbling of a brook. The authority of a lion's roar, the chirping of a cricket, the silent flutter of a butterfly's wings, the dancing birds in spring. The gentle falling of snowflakes, the powerful crashing of waves, the colorful transformation of leaves in fall, and the purple and orange hues in a sunset.

God's voice cries out through these and many more facets of nature.

What aspect of nature most speaks to you?

What does God say through that demonstration of His creativity?

The complexity of the creation demands a Creator. Through creation, we are drawn into relationship with and appreciation of our Creator.

If there is a specific time in which you felt especially close to God through nature, reflect on that time and remember the truths you learned about Him through that experience.

Whether you live in a big city or a small town, take a moment today to commune with God through nature. You can look up at the stars tonight, take a lunch break outside under a tree, go for a walk, or watch the rain fall against the window.

What is the Creator saying to you today? And how can you share that with others?

Luke 19:40 (ESV)

He answered, "I tell you, if these were silent, the very stones would cry out."

Additional notes, drawings, or thoughts from listening to the Creator today:

Week 2, Day 2
Hearing the Creator through His Ultimate Creation

"In the beginning God created the heavens and the earth" (Gen. 1:1). And throughout the following five days, the Creator created the marvelous and wondrous things we reflected on yesterday. Every aspect of creation proclaims His glory. And we are no exception.

The Creator saved the best two creations for last when He made man out of the dust of the ground, breathing life into Him, then formed woman from a rib taken out of man (Gen. 1:26-27, 31; 2:18-25).

The intricacies of the human body are a marvel. They definitely affirm the design of a creator. Where we differ from animals, and the most fascinating facet of all, is our minds—how our brains form, learn language, communicate, think, process, problem-solve, desire, dream, and perform daily functions.

The psalmist said in Psalm 139:13-16 (ESV):

> **¹³ For you formed my inward parts;**
>   **you knitted me together in my mother's womb.**
> **¹⁴ I praise you, for I am fearfully and wonderfully made.**
> **Wonderful are your works;**
>   **my soul knows it very well.**
> **¹⁵ My frame was not hidden from you,**
> **when I was being made in secret,**
>   **intricately woven in the depths of the earth.**
> **¹⁶ Your eyes saw my unformed substance;**
> **in your book were written, every one of them,**
>   **the days that were formed for me,**
>   **when as yet there was none of them.**

A contemplation of the marvels of the human body speaks to the wonder of our Creator. But our very words can also be a vessel used by Him to proclaim His glory and share His message.

Consider the following verses as they present an opportunity for us to serve as the voice of God to others who are listening.

Ephesians 5:19-20 (NIV)

[19] speaking to one another with psalms, hymns, and songs from the Spirit. Sing and make music from your heart to the Lord, [20] always giving thanks to God the Father for everything, in the name of our Lord Jesus Christ.

Mark 16:15 (ESV)

[15] And he said to them, "Go into all the world and proclaim the gospel to the whole creation."

Ephesians 4:15-16 (ESV)

[15] Rather, speaking the truth in love, we are to grow up in every way into him who is the head, into Christ, [16] from whom the whole body, joined and held together by every joint with which it is equipped, when each part is working properly, makes the body grow so that it builds itself up in love.

What is the Creator saying to you today through these verses?

Are you willing to be His vessel to allow someone else to hear Him? And are you open to hearing His voice through someone else?

One final reflection for additional study and listening: How do we discern whether what someone else is saying is from God or not? (Acts 17:11; 1 John 4:1-6)

Additional notes, drawings and thoughts from listening to the Creator today:

Week 2, Day 3
God Listened First

Made in God's image, we were designed to be in relationship. And our Creator modeled this relationship, starting in the Garden of Eden.

We are familiar with the story of the fall of man—sin entered the world when Adam and Eve disobeyed God's command. Today, we are going to focus on the interaction and relationship between the Creator and the created as seen in the following four verses: Genesis 3:8-11 (ESV).

⁸ And they heard the sound of the LORD God walking in the garden in the cool of the day, and the man and his wife hid themselves from the presence of the LORD God among the trees of the garden. ⁹ But the LORD God called to the man and said to him, "Where are you?" ¹⁰ And he said, "I heard the sound of you in the garden, and I was afraid, because I was naked, and I hid myself." ¹¹ He said, "Who told you that you were naked? Have you eaten of the tree of which I commanded you not to eat?"

What did Adam and Eve hear (v. 8)? What do you think it sounded like?

How do you think they reacted to the same sound before that day?

Why did they hide that time (Gen. 3:10)?

Do we ever hide when we don't want to listen to what we know we need to hear?

What do you think Adam and Eve expected to be the first words out of God's mouth?

What did God say?

But didn't God already know the answer?

After Adam answers the first question, God again asks a question to which He already knows the answer (v. 11). Why?

Listening is about relationship. Our Creator longs to be in relationship with us. He wants us to listen to Him (a practice we are learning), but He also wants to listen to us—to engage in conversation.

Today, even though God already knows what is on your heart, I encourage you to engage in conversation with Him through prayer.

Talk with the Creator. Allow Him to listen to you. And take turns listening to Him.

Additional thoughts, notes, or drawings from listening to the Creator:

Week 2, Day 4
The Potter Creates a Masterpiece

The Creator is not done yet. The following poem was a simple song I learned as a child in Sunday school. I encourage you to reflect on the words of that poem and the verse below as you color, or draw on the next page, the Potter's hand.

"He's still working on me,

To make me what I ought to be.

It took Him just a week to make the moon and stars,

The sun and the earth and Jupiter and Mars.

How loving and patient He must be...

For He's still working on me."

BUT *now*, O LORD,
THOU ART OUR FATHER;
WE ARE THE *clay*,
AND THOU OUR POTTER;
AND WE *all* ARE THE
work of thy hand.
ISAIAH 64:8

*Shall what is formed say to the one who formed it, "You did not make me"?
Can the pot say to the potter, "You know nothing"?*

Isaiah 29:16b

Week 2, Day 5
The Creator's Got This—He's in Control

The Creator got things started, but didn't just sit back and let it all spin out of control. He is *still* in control—a living and active God that has everything taken care of.

In order to meditate on this truth today and listen to the Creator's voice, we are going to go through the steps of the spiritual discipline known as *Lectio Divina*.[1] This discipline can be practiced with any portion of Scripture.

Before you start, spend some time in silence, preparing your mind to hear what God says to you through that passage of Scripture. Today, we want to pay special attention, listening to the Creator through His Word.

Read the chosen verses (Matt. 6:25-34, NIV, for today) four consecutive times. Each time you read it, you will ask a different question and will follow each step with another period of silence.

1. **Read** the passage listening for a word or phrase that jumps out at you. Savor and repeat the word without reflecting too much on it.

2. **Reflect** or meditate on the word or phrase while reading through the passage a second time. You might ask, "What is it in my life that needed to hear this word today?"

3. **Respond**. Is there an invitation or challenge that God is calling

---

[1] Portions taken from Sacred Rhythms by Ruth Haley Barton and Celebration of Discipline by Richard Foster.

you to? What is your response to this invitation? Perhaps this scripture has touched a place of pain, frustration, or anger. We can pour out these feelings in the safety of this moment of communion with God, and in prayer.

4. When our response has subsided, we read the passage one last time, in **contemplation**—to rest in God and resolve that we will walk with Him in our daily life, inspired and encouraged by the word or phrase that we have heard through this exercise.

Matthew 6:25-34 (NIV)

[25] "Therefore I tell you, do not worry about your life, what you will eat or drink; or about your body, what you will wear. Is not life more than food, and the body more than clothes? [26] Look at the birds of the air; they do not sow or reap or store away in barns, and yet your heavenly Father feeds them. Are you not much more valuable than they? [27] Can any one of you by worrying add a single hour to your life?

[28] And why do you worry about clothes? See how the flowers of the field grow. They do not labor or spin. [29] Yet I tell you that not even Solomon in all his splendor was dressed like one of these. [30] If that is how God clothes the grass of the field, which is here today and tomorrow is thrown into the fire, will he not much more clothe you—you of little faith? [31] So do not worry, saying, 'What shall we eat?' or 'What shall we drink?' or 'What shall we wear?' [32] For the pagans run after all these things, and your heavenly Father knows that you need them. [33] But seek first his kingdom and his righteousness, and all these things will be given to you as well. [34] Therefore do not worry about tomorrow, for tomorrow will worry about itself. Each day has enough trouble of its own.

Additional notes, drawings, or thoughts from listening to the Creator today:

Week 2, Day 6
The Still, Small Voice

We listen for what we want to hear. But what happens when the message is presented differently than we expected?

This happened to Elijah when he was hiding out in a cave. He was depressed and discouraged because Jezebel was chasing him—he was running for his life. And this cave-hiding moment happened right after he had witnessed God's demonstration of power against the prophets of Baal on Mount Carmel (1 Kings 18:20-40).

Read 1 Kings 19:9-18.

A low whisper; a sound; a thin silence; a still, small voice.

Translators have wrestled with how to interpret the voice and presence of God that day. Whatever it was, however Elijah might best describe it, he *knew* that God was speaking to him. And after all that had occurred in recent days and the running he had done, he was finally ready to listen.

Instead of focusing on what God said to Elijah that day, we are going to follow his example and **listen to the Creator through silence**.

Spend at least 5 minutes in total silence. Set a timer so that you aren't focused on how much time is left.

Your thoughts, your family, and other distractions may make this a difficult exercise. But every time the "noise" threatens, repeat, "I am listening to the still, small voice."

I will share no more thoughts and give no more direction for today's listening practice. I, too, am listening to the still, small voice.

Notes, drawings, or thoughts from listening to the still, small voice of the Creator:

Week 2, Day 7
The Creator Rested

Yesterday, we reflected in silence. Today, we will contemplate rest.

Genesis 2:2-3 (ESV)

² And on the seventh day God finished his work that he had done, and he rested on the seventh day from all his work that he had done. ³ So God blessed the seventh day and made it holy, because on it God rested from all his work that he had done in creation.

Following the lead of the Creator, and the commandment in Exodus 20:8-11, we are told to rest as a celebration of the work that has been done.

However, Deuteronomy presents a different facet of rest that connects with our focus on listening.

While we do not see the specifics of the Sabbath commanded in the New Testament, nor the direct command to keep the seventh day holy, the spirit and purposes of the Sabbath rest continue, which we will explore today. The Jewish teachers of the law had lost the spirit of the Sabbath rest, as commanded by God, which I hope we can renew a bit today.

Exodus 20:8-11 (ESV)

⁸ Remember the Sabbath day, to keep it holy. ⁹ Six days you shall labor, and do all your work, ¹⁰ but the seventh day is a Sabbath to the LORD your God. On it you shall not do any work, you, or your son, or your daughter, your male servant, or your female servant, or your livestock, or the sojourner who is within your gates. ¹¹ For in six days the LORD made heaven and earth, the sea,

and all that is in them, and rested on the seventh day. Therefore the LORD blessed the Sabbath day and made it holy.

According to the Exodus account, why were the Israelites commanded to rest (v.11)?

Now, let's look at the version of the Sabbath instructions in Deuteronomy 5:12-15 (ESV).

¹² Observe the Sabbath day, to keep it holy, as the LORD your God commanded you. ¹³ Six days you shall labor and do all your work, ¹⁴ but the seventh day is a Sabbath to the LORD your God. On it you shall not do any work, you or your son or your daughter or your male servant or your female servant, or your ox or your donkey or any of your livestock, or the sojourner who is within your gates, that your male servant and your female servant may rest as well as you. ¹⁵ You shall remember that you were a slave in the land of Egypt, and the LORD your God brought you out from there with a mighty hand and an outstretched arm. Therefore the LORD your God commanded you to keep the Sabbath day.

Focusing on verse 15, why are the Israelites commanded to rest? What is the purpose of their rest?

In Exodus, they rested from work (at the end of the week). In Deuteronomy, they rested in preparation for work (a time to remember God's faithfulness, rescue, and provision—mentally and spiritually preparing for the week to come).

The Creator rested. And He gave us two distinct purposes for our rest. He left us that example and that command. We can look at rest as a gift, rather than a reward.

What is the Creator saying to you about rest?

Additional notes, drawings, and thoughts from listening to the Creator:

Week 2: **Listening to the Creator**

Each week, when we gather together, we will share the ways in which we have listened, what we have heard, and how we can continue to encourage and inspire one another in our listening. We have dedicated a time each day to listen to God and now we will devote some time listening to one another.

The following are the two questions we will ask and answer together each week.

1) What have you heard from the Creator this week?

2) Which day's listening activity most resonated with you? And why that one?

Now, based on what we have each heard, we will share in the Common Threads (an Iron Rose Sister Ministries way of making any lesson, teaching, or reflection very personal and practical). The Common Threads help us focus in on the specifics of what we have heard and guide us into putting those things into practice, all in the context of community. They also serve as a form of spiritual journaling, which is why I encourage you to date them and look back later to see your growth.

Each woman's answers will be different because we hear unique things and each face different spiritual battles at any given moment. However, we can encourage one another to grow and bloom in those areas, remove thorns that hinder that growth, and hold each other accountable as iron sharpening iron.

Common Threads:

Date _____

An area in which you'd like to grow or bloom.

_____

_____

A thorn you'd like to remove.

_____

_____

An area in which you'd like to dig deeper or need someone to hold you accountable. (How can we, as a group, help you continue to listen or put into practice what you have heard?)

_____

_____

A message of hope, an encouraging word, or scripture from your time of listening.

_____

_____

Close each week in a time of prayer thanking God for what you have heard and bringing to God the requests shared through the Common Threads. This is an opportunity to join as one voice in our struggles, to rejoice in our victories, and to continue to listen to God and one another.

Week 3, Day 1
Listening through the Word

This week, we will be listening to God, the Father. Can we listen to the Father without going to His Word?

As we listen to and for the voice of God, let us remember the following truths:

Isaiah 40:8 (NIV)

8 The grass withers and the flowers fall,
  but the word of our God endures forever.

2 Peter 1:20-21 (NIV)

20 Above all, you must understand that no prophecy of Scripture came about by the prophet's own interpretation of things. 21 For prophecy never had its origin in the human will, but prophets, though human, spoke from God as they were carried along by the Holy Spirit.

He longs to instruct us, if we will listen...

2 Timothy 3:16-17 (ESV)

16 All Scripture is breathed out by God and profitable for teaching, for reproof, for correction, and for training in righteousness, 17 that the man of God may be complete, equipped for every good work.

Psalm 85:8 (ESV)

**Let me hear what God the Lord will speak,
for he will speak peace to his people, to his saints;
but let them not turn back to folly.**

For today, listening to the Word, choose one of the above verses (or a different verse of your choice) and write it out three times. Here are a variety of ideas for the three ways you can write it out:

1) Write it on a notecard and put it in your purse, car, or bathroom—a place you will see it and listen to the Father through His Word.
2) Draw your interpretation of the verse.
3) Look up another version of the verse and write it out.
4) Insert your own name into the verse as a prayer.
5) Put it to music.
6) Feel free to come up with your own idea!

Week 3, Day 2
Listen to *Who* He is, not just *What* He says

Be still and know that He is God.

Cease striving.

Stop fighting.

Psalm 46:10 expresses each of these sentiments.

God is in control. And if we will be still, cease striving, and stop fighting, we will know and remember that He is God.

However, my spirit is often far from still. I feel anxious. Questioning. Doubtful.

Focused on listening to the Father's voice, I have been disturbed by some of what I hear. Have I been so focused on my own thoughts and driven by my own desires—an interpretation of what I think God's will is for my life—that I have ceased listening?

Henri Nouwen said, "How sad it is that thinking often makes prayers cease."

And prayer is listening as much or more than it is speaking.

So I will be still. I will cease striving. I will stop fighting the war within me.

And I will KNOW that He is God.

Most of you know that I love languages. I call Spanish my nerdy passion and I enjoying being able to explore other cultures through their use of language.

There are some words that are more easily expressed in one language than another. And some words we don't attempt to say in our own language, but rather borrow them from another, like "bon appétit," or "quesadilla." Not all borrowed words refer to foods, like "déjà vu," or "Colorado" (meaning red-colored, a description of the river that runs through that state).

We are going to look at a Hebrew word and then two Spanish words as we listen to and come to know God today.

Notice that the following two translations of Exodus 14:14 interpret the final Hebrew word differently.

Exodus 14:14 (ESV)

¹⁴ The LORD will fight for you, and you have only to *be silent*.

Exodus 14:14 (NIV)

¹⁴ The LORD will fight for you; you need only to *be still*.

No words. No movement. The Hebrew captures the concept of stillness and silence in one word: *charash*. What is the correlation between being silent and being still?

Having presented the correlation between stillness and silence in listening to and coming to know God, I want to introduce you to two different Spanish words for "to know." Their distinct meanings will help highlight an important aspect of knowing God.

Saber is to know facts. *Conocer* is to know personally.

If you were to make a list of the top ten characteristics of God, what would your list look like?

While many of us would give a Sunday-school answer and be completely correct in our description, there is a difference between saying that we know something about God (saber) and knowing intimately that aspect of God through relationship or personal experience (conocer).

I know (saber) that God is the author of Scripture, but have I gotten to know (conocer) the living breathing Word of God?

I know (saber) that God is good, but how have I come to know (conocer) His goodness?

I may know a lot of things about God (saber), but am I intimately walking with Him in communication and relationship in order to know Him more (conocer)?

Now that we have looked at various aspects of the concepts: "being still" and "knowing," how can you "Be still and know that He is God" today?

Additional notes, drawings or thoughts from listening to the Father:

Week 3, Day 3
Listening for My Name

Fill in the following two blanks:

I am most excited to hear my name when it is called

_____

_____.

I most dread hearing my name when it is called

_____

_____.

John 10:3 (NIV)

The gatekeeper opens the gate for him, and the sheep listen to his voice. He calls his own sheep by name and leads them out.

My mom has a unique name. Not many people are named Jocelynn and if they are, they even more rarely have two N's at the end. When we hear her name, we immediately turn, thinking that it is in reference to my mom. We know her name and smile when we hear it spoken.

My name, however, is not as unique. At a family retreat in Cochabamba, Bolivia, there were three "Michelle"s in attendance: a toddler, a teen, and myself. Needless to say, the toddler was most often the Michelle being called, but I turned to look. Every. Single. Time.

And since I know that Michelle is not a unique name, I shouldn't be surprised when there is more than one Michelle around.

The funniest time there was a confusion of names was when I was in Bogota, Colombia, on a Sunday. There is a brother there named Michel (French for Michael, and how my name is pronounced in Spanish). So when the announcement came that Michel would be leading singing this morning, I froze, until I remembered that I was not the only "Michelle" in attendance.

Except for my moment of panic in Colombia, or the one time I was called to the principal's office as a kid, most of us like hearing our name called. Okay introverts, maybe you don't ever want the attention drawn to you by having your name called.

But, for better or worse, our name is part of who we are, and it is how we are known. Whether a nickname or the name on your birth certificate, it shapes who you are.

Many people have asked my dad if he is sad that his name will not be carried on to another generation since we are four daughters (no sons). He wisely replied that it mattered more to him that the name of Christ be what is passed on to the next generations.

With God as our Father, our name in Him is most important.

Romans 8:14-17 (ESV)

[14] For all who are led by the Spirit of God are sons of God. [15] For you did not receive the spirit of slavery to fall back into fear, but you have received the Spirit of adoption as sons, by whom we cry, "Abba! Father!" [16] The Spirit himself bears witness with our spirit that we are children of God, [17] and if children, then heirs—heirs of God and fellow heirs with Christ, provided we suffer with him in order that we may also be glorified with him.

Ephesians 1:3-6 (ESV)

[3] Blessed be the God and Father of our Lord Jesus Christ, who has blessed us in Christ with every spiritual blessing in the heavenly

places, ⁴even as he chose us in him before the foundation of the world, that we should be holy and blameless before him. In love ⁵he predestined us for adoption to himself as sons through Jesus Christ, according to the purpose of his will, ⁶to the praise of his glorious grace, with which he has blessed us in the Beloved.

1 Peter 1:2 (NLT)

²God the Father knew you and chose you long ago, and his Spirit has made you holy. As a result, you have obeyed him and have been cleansed by the blood of Jesus Christ. May God give you more and more grace and peace.

What does it mean to have the Father call you by name?

How do you feel knowing that He chose you?

What responsibility do we have as a child of God, bearing His name?

Additional notes, drawings, or thoughts from listening to the Father:

Week 3, Day 4
Listening Cleanly and Clearly—
And So I Listen.

What hinders our listening?

One of my own biggest hindrances is my own thoughts...

And so I listen.

My prayers have been transformed from a rambling conglomeration of words to moments of silence, listening to what God speaks to my heart. I have realized the value of being in the presence of the Lord instead of always feeling like I have to have something to say, or have the perfect words to express whatever is on my mind.

And so I listen to His heart.

After several years of friendship, while driving on a road trip, a friend commented, "I'm glad we have reached the point in our relationship where we don't feel like we have to fill the silence with noise. We are comfortable with ourselves, with each other, and with our relationship that it is enough to just be here together."

I think I have finally reached that point in my communication with God. He has more important things to say than I do. His wisdom is infinitely beyond mine. His thoughts are not my thoughts and His ways are not my ways (Isa. 55:8-9), yet I long for them to be more aligned.

And so I listen to His wisdom.

My desperate expression of needs never reaches the breadth and depth of His provision. The chorus of my prayers, when I am honest with my frustrations, returns to a sentiment of "not my will, but yours be done." So why don't I start there?

And so I listen to His will.

It's not that I have run out of words. I am still a verbose extrovert, eager for an audience. But I have weighed the value of listening, especially to God, and find it of greater worth than my own meager responses.

And so I listen to His voice.

And because I listen, I find that I actually have even more to say—more of His words, more of His Spirit, more of His heart, His desires, and His love.

And so I listen.

As you listen today, have a blank piece of paper with you. Jot down a reminder if your thoughts start to wander, so that you can set it aside and stay focused on your prayer time.

On the back of this page, we are going to write out our prayer today—it is a way of removing distractions and listening more, as we pray. (The blank piece of paper is to write down distracting thoughts and come back to your prayer, written in this book.)

Week 3, Day 5
Rebellious Ears Mean Broken Tears

Throughout the Old Testament, we hear the voice of God the Father more than that of the Son or the Spirit. And He spoke, most often, through prophets. However, the Israelites provided us with countless examples of those who did not listen... or if they listened, they did not obey.

When God speaks through Isaiah in chapter 48, He addresses the "house of Jacob, who are called by the name of Israel."

Isaiah 48:8, 17-19 (ESV)

⁸ You have never heard, you have never known,
  from of old your ear has not been opened.
For I knew that you would surely deal treacherously,
  and that from before birth you were called a rebel.

¹⁷ Thus says the LORD,
  your Redeemer, the Holy One of Israel:
"I am the LORD your God,
  who teaches you to profit,
  who leads you in the way you should go.
¹⁸ Oh that you had paid attention to my commandments!
  Then your peace would have been like a river,
  and your righteousness like the waves of the sea;
¹⁹ your offspring would have been like the sand,
  and your descendants like its grains;
their name would never be cut off
  or destroyed from before me."

What does God mean by they "have never heard" or "never known" (v. 8)?

What is the consequence of their not paying attention to His commandments (v. 17-19)?

I encourage you to read the entire chapter of Isaiah 48 as God expresses His frustration at their lack of attention to His instruction. This is, of course, not the only time that God gives such a description of Israel.

Ezekiel 12:1-2 (ESV)

The word of the LORD came to me: ²"Son of man, you dwell in the midst of a rebellious house, who have eyes to see, but see not, who have ears to hear, but hear not, for they are a rebellious house.

What happens when we do not listen to God's teaching?

What biblical example comes to mind of the pain or heartache associated with not listening to God?

What personal life example comes to mind?

What is the most important part of listening to God's commands?

Matthew 7:24-27 (NIV)

[24] "Therefore everyone who hears these words of mine and puts them into practice is like a wise man who built his house on the rock. [25] The rain came down, the streams rose, and the winds blew and beat against that house; yet it did not fall, because it had its foundation on the rock. [26] But everyone who hears these words of mine and does not put them into practice is like a foolish man who built his house on sand. [27] The rain came down, the streams rose, and the winds blew and beat against that house, and it fell with a great crash."

What is the difference between the wise and foolish builders? (Hint: they both heard the word.)

Additional notes, drawings, or thoughts from listening to the Father:

Week 3, Day 6
Called to Listen
through the Prophet Jeremiah

As someone who stays quite busy, whose thoughts are always whirling with a multi-tasked variety of ideas, calendars, commitments, and people, it is hard to stop and listen—to be fully present in the moment and listen. Listening to God, to others, and to the world.

The book of Jeremiah refers to listening or hearing more than any other book in the Bible. And it is in reference to God lamenting that His people have not listened to Him. I do not want to be the subject of our Father's lament. And I'm sure you don't either.

You have already made that choice by listening to the Father's voice throughout these forty days. For that, I congratulate you!

Read the following list of verses from the book of Jeremiah and as you listen, make note of:

1) The things that God wanted the Israelites to hear and
2) What He wants us to hear today.

Historical context: Jeremiah prophesied in Judah, just before the Babylonians took the nation into captivity.

Jeremiah 6:16-20

Jeremiah 7:1-8

Jeremiah 8:4-7

Jeremiah 9:23-24

Jeremiah 17:5-10

Jeremiah 18:5-10

Jeremiah 23:16-18

Jeremiah 29:10-14

Jeremiah 31:31-34

What is the overall message you hear from the Father through these passages?

Additional notes, thoughts, or drawings from listening to the Father:

Week 3, Day 7
Prophets → Christ → Spirit

Hebrews 1:1-2 (ESV)

Long ago, at many times and in many ways, God spoke to our fathers by the prophets, [2] but in these last days he has spoken to us by his Son, whom he appointed the heir of all things, through whom also he created the world.

This past week, we have been listening to the voice of the Father, most recently as He spoke through the prophets. Next week, we will focus on listening to Jesus, the Son. The following week, we will be listening to the Holy Spirit.

As we have seen, and are reminded by the author of Hebrews, God speaks in a plethora of ways, showing the importance He places on listening and how much He values communication in our relationship with Him.

And as the writer of Hebrews continues in chapter 2:1 (NIV):

We must pay the most careful attention, therefore, to what we have heard, so that we do not drift away.

Reflecting on the first half of our listening exercises (today starts Day 21 of 40), how have you heard God's voice?

What is the overarching, consistent message you have been hearing from the Father as Good Shepherd and Creator?

How has this transformed your relationship with God?

What do you hope to hear through the next half of our listening exercises?

Take some time in communion with the Father, thanking Him for the many ways in which He has spoken throughout history. **Thank Him** for the consistent messages He has always expressed—enumerate them, draw them, or celebrate them in song.

Week 3: **Listening to the Father**

Each week, when we gather together, we will share the ways in which we have listened, what we have heard, and how we can continue to encourage and inspire one another in our listening. We have dedicated a time each day to listen to God and now we will devote some time listening to one another.

The following are the two questions we will ask and answer together each week.

1) What have you heard from the Father this week?

2) Which day's listening activity most resonated with you? And why that one?

Now, based on what we have each heard, we will share in the Common Threads (an Iron Rose Sister Ministries way of making any lesson, teaching, or reflection very personal and practical). The Common Threads help us focus in on the specifics of what we have heard and guide us into putting those things into practice, all in the context of community. They also serve as a form of spiritual journaling, which is why I encourage you to date them and look back later to see your growth.

Each woman's answers will be different because we hear unique things and each face different spiritual battles at any given moment. However, we can encourage one another to grow and bloom in those areas, remove thorns that hinder that growth, and hold each other accountable as iron sharpening iron.

Common Threads:

Date _____

An area in which you'd like to grow or bloom.

_____

_____

A thorn you'd like to remove.

_____

_____

An area in which you'd like to dig deeper or need someone to hold you accountable. (How can we, as a group, help you continue to listen or put into practice what you have heard?)

_____

_____

A message of hope, an encouraging word, or scripture from your time of listening.

_____

_____

Close each week in a time of prayer thanking God for what you have heard and bringing to God the requests shared through the Common Threads. This is an opportunity to join as one voice in our struggles, to rejoice in our victories, and to continue to listen to God and one another.

Week 4, Day 1
Make the Way Straight and Welcome

O ne cannot listen as clearly when there is interference. A muffled sound creates confusion and doubt regarding the clarity of the message.

When John the Baptist came onto the scene, the priests and Levites were sent to ask him who he was and what he was doing. John affirmed that his purpose was in fulfillment of the prophecy in Isaiah, "a voice crying out in the wilderness, 'make straight the way of the Lord'" (John 1:23, ESV).

What does it mean to make straight the way of the Lord?

When building a normal road, the twists and turns, rises and falls of the road follow the lay of the land and the curve of the mountains. However, when a road is prepared for royalty, the way is made straight. Mountains are moved, curves are straightened, the path made smooth.

When we prepare our listening ears, how can we make the way straight for the Lord?

One idea is to welcome Him as King like the Jews did upon entering Jerusalem (Matt. 21:5-11, ESV).

⁵ "Say to the daughter of Zion,
'Behold, your king is coming to you,
    humble, and mounted on a donkey,
    on a colt, the foal of a beast of burden.'"
⁶ The disciples went and did as Jesus had directed them. ⁷ They brought the donkey and the colt and put on them their cloaks, and he sat on them. ⁸ Most of the crowd spread their cloaks on the road, and others cut branches from the trees and spread them on the road. ⁹ And the crowds that went before him and that followed him were shouting, "Hosanna to the Son of David! Blessed is he who comes in the name of the Lord! Hosanna in the highest!" ¹⁰ And when he entered Jerusalem, the whole city was stirred up, saying, "Who is this?" ¹¹ And the crowds said, "This is the prophet Jesus, from Nazareth of Galilee."

On the next page, there is a blank palm branch with the word Hosanna. Hosanna means "adoration, praise or joy." In a spirit of praise and with an attitude of listening, we are going to lay our burdens and our thanksgivings at His feet. In the leaves of the branch, write things that you are thankful for, or burdens you are carrying. Picture yourself laying these branches before Him and giving it over to Him. We are making the way straight; we are opening the path to our hearts. We are removing any obstacles; we are opening our ears. We are welcoming the King of Kings as Lord of our life and speaker of truth. Blessed is He who comes in the name of the Lord.

Additional notes, drawings, or thoughts from listening to the Son:

Week 4, Day 2
Only Speak What the Father Has Told Me / You Have Heard that It is Said...

Jesus had a lot to say. But He knew what to say, when to say it, how to say it, and when to keep silent. What wisdom!

John 12:49 (ESV)

⁴⁹ For I have not spoken on my own authority, but the Father who sent me has himself given me a commandment—what to say and what to speak.

How was Jesus able to speak only His Father's words and remain clear in what the Father intended for His people to hear?

The Son of God made it a priority to set aside time in communication with His Father. In Luke 6:12, we see that Jesus "went out to the mountain to pray and spent all night in prayer to God." All. Night.

The Son of God, who was one with the Father, spent all night in communication with Him. How does that reflect the importance of spending time talking and listening to the Father?

Like the teachers of the law, many of us fall into the trap of not listening—or sticking stubbornly to what we thought we heard the first time. They had lost the spirit of all God had taught them through the commandments. Throughout the Sermon on the Mount, Jesus rectifies the errant teaching and clarifies the truth of God's message to His people.

"You have heard that it is said, but I tell you..." There were a number of things that the Israelites had gotten all wrong. And before we quickly condemn them, we must recognize our confusion at some of God's teaching as well. We listen through the filter of past understanding or current circumstances and muddy the waters of His clear message.

Today, we are going to listen with fresh ears to the Sermon on the Mount in Matthew 5-7. Picture yourself sitting at the feet of Jesus on the mountainside as He first taught. Read these chapters while asking the following questions:

How do I hear these words of Jesus with new perspective?

Even if "I've heard that it is said," what do I need to listen to today?

Notes, drawings or thoughts from listening to the Son through the Sermon on the Mount:

Evidenced in the Sermon on the Mount, Jesus was clear in His purpose while on earth—even if what He needed to say was not what others wanted to hear. Consider the following verses as filters through which we consider the words we speak. Jesus kept these things in mind as He spoke to His Father and to others.

Matthew 22:34-40

Matthew 26:42

After listening to these verses, make note (above) of what you hear God saying and how He might want you to communicate those truths to others, using Christ's example.

Week 4, Day 3
Sin-clogged ears

My hearing was excellent. Or so I thought. While in college, I had my ears checked and the audiologist informed me that my hearing was not as stellar as I had projected. She further clarified that part of my problem was the wax buildup clogging my ear canal.

Not knowing that my ears were clogged, my pride mirrored the waxy hindrance to my listening. I was so confident that my hearing was just fine that I was not open to hearing that there was any problem.

The Pharisees and teachers of the law had a similar problem. And the strongest admonition or tongue-lashing that Jesus issued was to the sin-clogged ears of this group of people.

Christ's language in Matthew 23 is clear and uncompromising in His disdain for their hypocritical actions and attitudes (v. 27-28, ESV).

[27] **Woe to you, scribes and Pharisees, hypocrites! For you are like whitewashed tombs, which outwardly appear beautiful, but within are full of dead people's bones and all uncleanness. [28] So you also outwardly appear righteous to others, but within you are full of hypocrisy and lawlessness.**

Jesus sat and ate with the sinners, tax collectors, and less-reputable members of society not because they were perfect. Rather, they admitted their sinful condition and did not allow that sin to clog their listening ears.

Confession is powerful as it brings sin to light and allows God to work His power of transformation in our lives.

Today's prayer of listening comes from Psalm 139:23-24 (NIV).

23 Search me, God, and know my heart;
  test me and know my anxious thoughts.
24 See if there is any offensive way in me,
  and lead me in the way everlasting.

As you pray this prayer today, imagine yourself visiting the Great Physician and asking Him to clean out your sin-clogged ears. Pretend you are Zacchaeus (Luke 19). Jesus has invited Himself over for a cup of coffee and His very presence convicts you in a loving way, inspiring you to confess and repent.

Below, write out your own prayer, possibly a prayer a confession, inspired by today's listening.

Additional notes, drawings, or thoughts from listening to the Son:

Week 4, Day 4
Red Letter Edition

In order to emphasize the priority of listening more attentively to the words of the Son, some editions of the Bible present all words spoken by Jesus, printed in red letters. Today's listening exercise is thus referred to as the "Red Letter Edition," because we will be listening only to the words of the Son.

Read the following words of Jesus as He demonstrates His authority, compassion, power, and love. Listen to His words as they were spoken during His time here on earth and picture Him saying them to you today. We already looked at His seven "I AM" statements from the book of John during week 1, so today, we will focus on some of His sayings in Matthew, Mark, and Luke.

"You of little faith, why are you so afraid?" (Matt. 8:26)

"Follow me" (Matt. 9:9).

"Do you believe I am able to do this?" (Matt. 9:28)

"Do not be afraid..." (three times in Matt. 10:26-30).

"Come to me, all you who are weary and burdened, and I will give you rest. Take my yoke upon you and learn from me, for I am gentle and humble in heart, and you will find rest for your souls. For my yoke is easy and my burden is light" (Matt. 11:28-30).

"My Father, if it is possible, may this cup be taken from me. Yet not as I will, but as you will" (Matt. 26:39).

"Watch and pray so that you will not fall into temptation. The spirit is willing, but the body is weak" (Matt. 26:41).

"I am willing," he said, *"Be clean!"* (Mark 1:41)

"Quiet! Be still!" (to the winds and the waves, Mark 4:39)

"Daughter, your faith has healed you. Go in peace and be freed from your suffering" (to the woman who had been bleeding for 12 years, Mark 5:34).

"Everything is possible for him who believes" (Mark 9:23).

"Take it; this is my body... This is my blood of the covenant..." (Mark 14:22, 24).

"Why were you searching for me?" he asked. *"Didn't you know I had to be in my Father's house?"* (Luke 2:49)

"Be quiet!" Jesus said sternly. *"Come out of him!"* (to a demon, Luke 4:35)

"Don't cry" (to a widow who lost her son, Luke 7:13).

"What do you want me to do for you?" (Luke 18:41)

"For the Son of Man came to seek and to save what was lost" (Luke 19:10).

"Well done my good and faithful servant" (Luke 19:17).

"Father, forgive them, for they do not know what they are doing" (Luke 23:34).

Which sayings of Jesus did you most need to listen to today?

Additional notes, thoughts, or drawings from listening to the words of the Son:

Week 4, Day 5
Listening in Layers

Jesus taught in parables. He wanted us to understand on a deeper level and He realized that we would not all be at the point of comprehending the layers of His teaching all at once.

The Parable of the Sower is an excellent example of Jesus' style of teaching, especially as He responds to the apostles' question regarding His chosen style.

Read Matthew 13:1-23.

Whether this is your first or twenty-first time reading the parable, what aspect of it jumps out at you today?

What is the application for the farmer who plants a seed?

What is the application for us as sowers of the seed?

Going back to verses 10-17, why does Jesus teach in parables?

Based on what you have heard through this parable today, what is your prayer, in thanksgiving or request, on your behalf and on behalf of others? Be sure to listen to Jesus' heart and His desire through this parable, in expressing your prayers.

Additional notes, drawings, or thoughts from listening to the Son:

Week 4, Day 6
Listening at the Feet of the Cross

Today, we are listening through music. Whether or not you know the following hymn, reflect on the words as a promise of truth. For me, this listening exercise was most impactful when I pictured myself singing in front of the empty cross. And don't forget to proclaim this truth-filled promise to others.

Feel free to make notes in and around the blank cross on the next page, as you listen to the Son, our Redeemer.

<u>I Know that My Redeemer Lives</u>, *by Fred A. Filmore*

> I know that my Redeemer lives,
> And ever prays for me;
> I know eternal life He gives,
> From sin and sorrow free.
>
> *Chorus*
> *I know, I know that my Redeemer lives,*
> *I know, I know eternal life He gives;*
> *I know, I know that my Redeemer lives.*
>
> He wills that I should holy be,
> In word, in tho't, in deed;
> Then I His holy face may see,
> When from this earth-life freed.
> *Chorus*

I know that unto sinful men
His saving grace is nigh;
I know that He will come again
To take me home on high.
Chorus

I know that over yonder stands
A place prepared for me;
A home, a house not made with hands,
Most wonderful to see.
Chorus

Week 4, Day 7
It's a Matter of Perspective

Compliments and cut downs. Constructive criticism and complaints. For good or for ill, we hear what we want to hear—or at least what we think we have heard.

If someone offers a compliment, we may not hear it in the spirit it was shared. The tone of voice, speaker, timing, and many other factors play into our interpretation of the other person's words.

We filter our listening through our perceptions, our past experiences, and our warped understanding. Two people can say the exact same thing, but we hear it better from one person than from the other.

We also hear things better when they are presented from a different angle or highlight things in a way we can more easily understand.

Matthew, Mark, Luke and John did that. They each shared the story of Jesus, but did so with different audiences and perspectives in mind.

Why do we have the gospel story shared in four different books?

Matthew wrote to the Jews about Jesus, the Messiah—the fulfillment of the prophecies and the One who established the kingdom.

Mark gave an action-packed account of how the people were amazed at all Jesus did.

Luke chose a more Gentile audience who was not familiar with the Jewish traditions and longed to hear other details highlighted during Jesus' time on earth.

John focused more on who Jesus is and all He represents as the great I AM, the Word that became flesh and dwelt among us.

Each of the four gospels provides unique insight into Jesus and His time on earth. At different times in my life, one of those unique perspectives has spoken to me more than another.

A small group Bible study member once compared the gospels to four different puzzles. They each display a different picture and if you try to fit the pieces of one puzzle into the frame of another, it doesn't work.

John presents a more thematic than chronological approach, for example. And since Luke is speaking to the Gentiles and Matthew to the Jews, their views on different events are seen from distinct directions.

What a blessing that we have these four accounts of our Savior's time on earth! The story of Christ would be incomplete if we didn't have these four perspectives.

Which perspective most resonates with you currently, or which one do you feel you most need to listen to?

Jesus did not hesitate to say exactly what needed to be said, do what needed to be done, teach what needed to be taught, or clarify what had been confused. He did not cater to what others' itching ears needed to hear. However, He did consider His audience.

Read these four versions of the same story, as found in the four gospels. We can use a similar approach to listening when we refer to different versions or translations of the Bible. If you notice any differences or apparent discrepancies, listen to them as unique perspectives and insights.

Matthew 20:20-28

Mark 10:35-45

Luke 22:24-27

John 13:12-17

Additional notes, thoughts or drawings from listening to the Son:

Week 4: **Listening to the Son**

E ach week, when we gather together, we will share the ways in which we have listened, what we have heard, and how we can continue to encourage and inspire one another in our listening. We have dedicated a time each day to listen to God and now we will devote some time listening to one another.

The following are the two questions we will ask and answer together each week.

1) What have you heard from the Son this week?

2) Which day's listening activity most resonated with you? And why that one?

Now, based on what we have each heard, we will share in the Common Threads (an Iron Rose Sister Ministries way of making any lesson, teaching, or reflection very personal and practical). The Common Threads help us focus in on the specifics of what we have heard and guide us into putting those things into practice, all in the context of community. They also serve as a form of spiritual journaling, which is why I encourage you to date them and look back later to see your growth.

Each woman's answers will be different because we hear unique things and each face different spiritual battles at any given moment. However, we can encourage one another to grow and bloom in those areas, remove thorns that hinder that growth, and hold each other accountable as iron sharpening iron.

Common Threads:

Date _____

An area in which you'd like to grow or bloom.

_____

_____

A thorn you'd like to remove.

_____

_____

An area in which you'd like to dig deeper or need someone to hold you accountable. (How can we, as a group, help you continue to listen or put into practice what you have heard?)

_____

_____

A message of hope, an encouraging word, or scripture from your time of listening.

_____

_____

Close each week in a time of prayer thanking God for what you have heard and bringing to God the requests shared through the Common Threads. This is an opportunity to join as one voice in our struggles, to rejoice in our victories, and to continue to listen to God and one another.

Week 5, Day 1
How the Spirit Speaks and Listens

In the Old Testament, the Spirit was more of a silent partner (Gen. 1:2). God anointed a few choice individuals with His Spirit, some with a double portion (2 Kings 2:9). And then the Spirit carried along the prophets and the writers of the Bible, as we know it today (2 Pet. 1:21, ESV).

21 For no prophecy was ever produced by the will of man, but men spoke from God as they were carried along by the Holy Spirit.

Now that Christ has come and was raised, we each have the opportunity to walk intimately with the Spirit—even have Him dwelling in us!

When and how are we anointed with the Spirit? *Be sure and include specific scriptures to answer this question.*

How does the Spirit speak today?

Read John 15:26-27, 16:7-15. From these verses in John, list five characteristics of the Spirit and His role in our listening.

What does Romans 8:26-27 (ESV) say about the Spirit's listening and speaking?

²⁶ Likewise the Spirit helps us in our weakness. For we do not know what to pray for as we ought, but the Spirit himself intercedes for us with groanings too deep for words. ²⁷ And he who searches hearts knows what is the mind of the Spirit, because the Spirit intercedes for the saints according to the will of God.

As the Spirit searches your heart and intercedes for you, take some time today to thank God for the Spirit that listens and speaks. If you don't have the words, call on the Spirit to speak for you. We can claim these promises!

How have you heard the Spirit speak to you? Have you felt its gentle nudging? Did you answer that call or ignore it? Make notes about that time, especially if are willing to share the story when you gather with your Iron Rose Sisters.

If you have not ever felt that the Spirit has spoken to you or led you, now is a good time to ask Him to speak—let Him know that you are listening.

Additional thoughts, notes, or drawings from listening to the Spirit:

Week 5, Day 2
"Speak for your servant is listening"

Hannah poured out her heart to God and He heard her cries. Eli thought she was drunk, but God was listening.

Read 1 Samuel 1:21-28.

What was the relationship between Samuel and Eli?

Now read 1 Samuel 3:1-21.

What happened on that night in 1 Samuel 3?

What did Samuel do when he didn't recognize the voice calling out to him?

How can we apply the same practice for listening today?

Who do you have in your life that has developed the practice of listening to God and His Spirit—has learned to recognize His voice? How have they developed that skill?

Today's prayer comes from Eli's suggestion and Samuel's words: "Speak for your servant is listening."

You are learning to recognize when and how the Spirit speaks in your life. And even when the voice is unclear, we can call out to Him and invite His words. "Speak for your servant is listening."

Additional notes, drawings, or thoughts from listening to the Spirit:

Week 5, Day 3
Listening to and for wisdom

The Holy Spirit leads us into all truth and, as a Counselor and Guide, directs us on a wise path. Wisdom can seem like an elusive concept. We may not have the opportunity to be as wise as Solomon, but James 1:5 promises that if any of us lacks wisdom, we can ask for it and God promises to give it.

The book of Proverbs is filled with descriptions of the merits of wisdom, warnings against rejecting it, and images portraying of the value of wisdom. Wisdom, knowledge, and understanding are often used interchangeably in the book.

Proverbs 8 gives us a personification of wisdom. Wisdom itself is speaking. Read the entire chapter and notice the language with which wisdom speaks.

Make note of phrases that jump out at you.

Sketch or summarize the points you see wisdom making.

And then answer the following questions:

Who/what does wisdom align herself with?

Who/what does wisdom hate or detest?

Looking back at verses 22-31, who/what else could be speaking? (Hint: Who are we listening to this week?)

What do wisdom and the Holy Spirit have in common?

Additional notes, thoughts, or drawings from listening to wisdom and the Holy Spirit:

Week 5, Day 4
Listen First and Twice

A s we highlighted while listening to the Creator, God listened to Adam. He desired to engage in conversation with His people, and still does!

James 1:19 (NIV) gives us a formula for listening.

My dear brothers and sisters, take note of this: Everyone should be quick to listen, slow to speak and slow to become angry,

And our anatomy gives us another reminder for listening: How many ears do we have? _____ And how many mouths? _____

James' recommendation applies to our communication with God and also with others. A wise missionary once phrased it this way as a reminder when meeting someone with whom you are studying the Bible: "You've got to let the other person empty their bucket. Listen to what they have to say and let them tell their story. Then you will know better how to respond to their doubts, answer their questions with Scripture, and know where they are coming from. How can you know where to begin the study if you don't know where they are starting from?"

Proverbs 18:13 (ESV)

**If one gives an answer before he hears,
it is his folly and shame.**

Thoughts about listening first and twice when talking with others:

The same practice is true in our communication with God.

Ecclesiastes 5:1-2 (ESV)

Guard your steps when you go to the house of God. To draw near to listen is better than to offer the sacrifice of fools, for they do not know that they are doing evil. ² Be not rash with your mouth, nor let your heart be hasty to utter a word before God, for God is in heaven and you are on earth. Therefore let your words be few.

God is infinitely wise. His thoughts are not our thoughts. His ways are not our ways (Is. 55:8-9). What does it look like to listen first and twice in prayer?

As you pray today, listening first and twice, may your prayer be an echo of Christ's prayer in the garden: "Not my will but yours be done" (Matt. 26:39). The Spirit will help you in this listening prayer. May we be slow to speak (James 1:19) and may our words be few (Eccl. 5:2).

Additional notes, thoughts, or drawings from listening to the Spirit:

Week 5, Day 5
Too Busy to Listen

I seem to never have time to do many of the things that are important to me. There are only 24 hours in a day, and I can fill them up quickly. Sometimes, my day is filled with all the right priorities. Other days, Netflix draws me into one more episode, scrolling through Facebook takes a twenty-minute chunk out of my day... my "too busy to listen" is really an excuse—an inaccurate description of my day because I have gotten lost in things that are not my highest priority. What is your excuse?

Matthew 6:33 (ESV)

33 But seek first the kingdom of God and his righteousness, and all these things will be added to you.

Making sure God is the highest priority in our time, in our relationships, and in our listening is tough. It doesn't happen without effort and intentionality. Listening requires discipline. It is like a muscle we must exercise. And when we don't practice our listening exercises, our spiritual muscles weaken and we have to work harder again to re-learn to listen.

During week 2, we practiced listening in silence. You were asked to sit still for five minutes and listen. When other thoughts creeped in, we repeated the phrase, "I'm listening to the still, small voice."

Today, we are going to use a similar practice throughout the entire day, inspired by Mary, Martha's sister, who *"sat at the Lord's feet and listened to his teaching"* (Lk. 10:39, ESV).

(For those with physical limitations, you can create a modified version of this listening exercise.)

Three different times today, sit on the floor for at least two minutes at a time, and picture yourself at the Lord's feet, listening. Invite the Spirit to speak to you through quiet reflection, reminding you of truth from the verses we have read together this week, or other scripture on which you are meditating. Remembering is one of the Spirit's special roles. We are going to invite Him to help us remember today.

At least three times today, we are going to intentionally pause to listen and remember.

Listen to His voice.

Remember His truths in Scripture.

Listen in silence.

Remember the countless blessings.

Additional notes, thoughts, or drawings from listening to the Spirit today:

Week 5, Day 6
He Who Has Ears to Hear—
Not Afraid to Listen

A gentleman went to the doctor and asked for advice on how to convince his wife to come in and have her hearing checked. The husband's frustration with his wife's lack of attention to what he had to say was growing, and he needed some assistance.

The doctor recommended that the man, upon returning home, stand about 15 feet away from his wife and ask her a question. If she didn't answer, stand about 10 feet away. And if there was still no response, move to about 5 feet away and repeat the question.

The gentleman decided this was a good strategy and agreed to try it. "Thanks, doc! Hopefully, I'll be bringing her in for that hearing check later this week."

When he got to the house, the husband greeted his wife and then stood the fifteen feet away and asked, "Honey, what's for dinner?" Nothing.

Moving to 10 feet away, he repeated the question. "Honey, what's for dinner?" Still nothing.

Now standing five feet away, after restating his question, his wife turned around and responded, "For the third time, we're having rice and beans. Now how did that doctor appointment go?"

When we have frustrations in communication, we react, thinking that the other person is the one with the hearing problem. We read the verses admonishing, "He who has ears to hear, let him hear..." But our response is, "I wish sister so-and-so would open her ears to the truth." However, the first assessment should always be to check our own ears.

No matter how true the statement or good the news, we can fall into the trap of seeking only to listen to what our itching ears want to hear.

2 Timothy 4:2-4 (ESV)

² preach the word; be ready in season and out of season; reprove, rebuke, and exhort, with complete patience and teaching. ³ For the time is coming when people will not endure sound teaching, but having itching ears they will accumulate for themselves teachers to suit their own passions, ⁴ and will turn away from listening to the truth and wander off into myths.

Today's prayer for listening is that the Spirit will open our ears and our heart to hear exactly what He wants us to hear. You may be tempted to pray that prayer over someone else—that God will open his/her ears and heart. It is a valid prayer, but we can only control our own listening, not anyone else's.

Why do we avoid listening?

I admit that, at times, I am afraid to listen. I avoid going to the Word, fearful of what God may reveal in my life or the pain of conviction that may come from what I hear.

Yet there is a difference between feeling convicted and being condemned. When we don't hear what our itching ears want to hear, rather listen to what God needs to say, our toes may get stepped on. But these words are spoken out of love, for our own good.

When the Spirit came on the apostles at the Day of Pentecost, they were inspired to speak as God directed. The Spirit equipped them to speak in the languages of all of the people present. And even though the message was convicting, what did it lead the people to?

Acts 2:36-41 (ESV)

[36] "Let all the house of Israel therefore know for certain that God has made him both Lord and Christ, this Jesus whom you crucified." [37] Now when they heard this they were cut to the heart, and said to Peter and the rest of the apostles, "Brothers, what shall we do?" [38] And Peter said to them, "Repent and be baptized every one of you in the name of Jesus Christ for the forgiveness of your sins, and you will receive the gift of the Holy Spirit. [39] For the promise is for you and for your children and for all who are far off, everyone whom the Lord our God calls to himself." [40] And with many other words he bore witness and continued to exhort them, saying, "Save yourselves from this crooked generation." [41] So those who received his word were baptized, and there were added that day about three thousand souls.

Repentance. An opportunity to begin anew. May we not cling to what our itching ears want to hear, but rather listen for the truth—even if it means we are cut to the heart.

Additional notes, thoughts, or drawings from listening to the Spirit:

Week 5, Day 7
Our Personal "Hearing Aid"

As has become evident throughout this week's listening exercises, an important part of listening is remembering what you hear. The Holy Spirit serves as our personal listening assistant or "hearing aid," especially when we forget what we have been told, just as we read in the verses from John earlier this week.

As we keep in step with the Spirit (Gal. 5:25), we will reflect the fruit of the Spirit (v. 22-23) and improve our listening.

How does each facet of the fruit of the Spirit aid us in our listening, to God and to one another?

Feel free to draw, write, or quote other Bible verses as part of your answer.

Love

Joy

Peace

Patience

Kindness

Goodness

Faithfulness

Gentleness

Self-Control

Additional notes, thoughts, or drawings from listening to the Spirit and contemplating His fruit:

Week 5: **Listening to the Spirit**

Each week, when we gather together, we will share the ways in which we have listened, what we have heard, and how we can continue to encourage and inspire one another in our listening. We have dedicated a time each day to listen to God and now we will devote some time listening to one another.

The following are the two questions we will ask and answer together each week.

1) What have you heard from the Holy Spirit this week?

2) Which day's listening activity most resonated with you? And why that one?

Now, based on what we have each heard, we will share in the Common Threads (an Iron Rose Sister Ministries way of making any lesson, teaching, or reflection very personal and practical). The Common Threads help us focus in on the specifics of what we have heard and guide us into putting those things into practice, all in the context of community. They also serve as a form of spiritual journaling, which is why I encourage you to date them and look back later to see your growth.

Each woman's answers will be different because we hear unique things and each face different spiritual battles at any given moment. However, we can encourage one another to grow and bloom in those areas, remove thorns that hinder that growth, and hold each other accountable as iron sharpening iron.

Common Threads:

Date _____

An area in which you'd like to grow or bloom.

_____

_____

A thorn you'd like to remove.

_____

_____

An area in which you'd like to dig deeper or need someone to hold you accountable. (How can we, as a group, help you continue to listen or put into practice what you have heard?)

_____

_____

A message of hope, an encouraging word, or scripture from your time of listening.

_____

_____

Close each week in a time of prayer thanking God for what you have heard and bringing to God the requests shared through the Common Threads. This is an opportunity to join as one voice in our struggles, to rejoice in our victories, and to continue to listen to God and one another.

Week 6, Day 1
Taste and See that the Lord is Good

Psalm 34:8 (ESV)

> Oh, taste and see that the Lord is good!
> Blessed is the man who takes refuge in him!

On a cold Friday morning in January, I took a moment to listen to the snow fall. You may think it has no sound, but that was the beauty of the stillness on that winter morning.

I stepped away from the buzz of my hard drive, the melodious ring of my phone, and the ping of notifications that demanded my attention. All of those things could wait.

Just as my yard was made new by a blanket of snow, my perspective on life and all my frustrations were made new from my time alone with God, listening to the snow fall.

In order to truly and fully listen, I engaged all of my senses. I love the smell of fresh snow and the texture is fun to feel, even on my gloved hands. The crunch under my feet adds to the sound of it falling, but only if I listen carefully through the red hat I have pulled tightly over my ears.

Watching the flakes fall of all different weights and sizes, I am enamored by the ones caught by the wind—the ones that tumble through the sky as they fall to the ground. Makes it harder to catch one to taste, but I love the way it melts on my tongue and moistens my breath.

Can you hear and taste the snow with me? Are you listening?

Listening is more than hearing a sound.

Growing up, my parents used to say, "I need you to listen with your eyes." They were calling for our full and undivided attention.

Listening takes place through all five senses, which is our focus for this week's listening exercises.

Today, as you savor that perfect cup of coffee, sip of tea, or morsel of food, may you be reminded to "taste and see that the Lord is good" (Ps. 34:8).

James 1:17 (ESV)

¹⁷ Every good gift and every perfect gift is from above, coming down from the Father of lights, with whom there is no variation or shadow due to change.

What does it mean to you to taste and see that the Lord is good?

How does taste connect to our practice of listening?

Additional thoughts, notes, or drawings from listening through the sense of taste:

Week 6, Day 2
Watch and Listen

What do you see when you intently listen to someone? You may be looking them in the eye, but you are also taking in social cues from their body language.

When I listen to God through Scripture, I read the words on the page and my eyes process the message I have been called to hear.

And when I see something that captures my attention, I am drawn to it, as an invitation to listen.

Moses was called to listen by first seeing what God had put before him.

Exodus 3:1-6 (NIV)

Now Moses was tending the flock of Jethro his father-in-law, the priest of Midian, and he led the flock to the far side of the wilderness and came to Horeb, the mountain of God. ²There the angel of the LORD appeared to him in flames of fire from within a bush. Moses saw that though the bush was on fire it did not burn up. ³So Moses thought, "I will go over and see this strange sight—why the bush does not burn up."
⁴When the LORD saw that he had gone over to look, God called to him from within the bush, "Moses! Moses!"
And Moses said, "Here I am."
⁵"Do not come any closer," God said. "Take off your sandals, for the place where you are standing is holy ground." ⁶Then he said, "I am the God of your father, the God of Abraham, the God of Isaac and the God of Jacob." At this, Moses hid his face, because he was afraid to look at God.

What do you notice as the sequence and relationship between seeing and listening in this story?

We can also describe it as the difference between active and passive listening. When we are actively striving to listen, we will be paying full attention to what God is saying. We will approach Him to listen and respond, sometimes based on what we have seen. Are you watching to listen?

How has God spoken to you through what you have seen? Or how you have observed God working in your life or in the lives of others?

What did God say when you watched and listened?

The more we watch, and the more we listen, the more ready we are to hear Him clearly the next time!

I'm honored to watch and listen together with you through these listening exercises.

Additional notes, thoughts, or drawings from listening by watching:

Week 6, Day 3
We are Always Listening to Something

My dad was plagued with a severe ear infection that suddenly and without warning turned into meningitis, sepsis, and pneumonia. He was in the hospital for a week, and then continued on IV antibiotics for ten days.

During that time, and for a few more weeks following, his right ear was totally blocked. Since he could hear no outside noise, his brain filled in the gap by providing its own soundtrack.

For about a month, dad heard full orchestral music, big band music, and an occasional oldie from back in the day. The song he always came back to was Rhapsody in Blue by George Gershwin— a great song and a classic, catchy tune.

We joked that it was a good thing he only listened to good music because what he "heard" during that time came from his brain, not from the sound waves we use in order to normally process sound.

As I reflected on this phenomenon, I realized, *we are always listening to something,* even if it is just the voice in our own head. There is no such thing as total silence. If we are in a quiet environment, our brains will compensate and our thoughts will bring their own "noise" to the moment.

Today, we will listen through our sense of hearing, but we will listen through silence.

Psalm 62:1-2, 5-8 (ESV)

**For God alone my soul waits in silence;
from him comes my salvation.**

[2] He alone is my rock and my salvation,
  my fortress; I shall not be greatly shaken.

[5] For God alone, O my soul, wait in silence,
  for my hope is from him.
[6] He only is my rock and my salvation,
  my fortress; I shall not be shaken.
[7] On God rests my salvation and my glory;
  my mighty rock, my refuge is God.
[8] Trust in him at all times, O people;
  pour out your heart before him;
  God is a refuge for us. *Selah*

Habakkuk 2:20 (ESV)

[20] But the Lord is in his holy temple;
  let all the earth keep silence before him.

Revelation 8:1 (ESV)

When the Lamb opened the seventh seal, there was silence in heaven for about half an hour.

We have become more practiced at listening through silence... I challenge you to listen for a half hour in silence. Picture yourself entering His holy temple and keeping silence before Him during that time. You may even sing the song inspired by the verse in Habakkuk, as you enter into the time of silence.

Additional notes, thoughts, or drawings from listening through the sense of hearing:

Week 6, Day 4
Not Even a Hint of Smoke

Smell is one of our strongest memory senses: fresh baked cookies at Grandma's house, honeysuckle in Louisiana each spring, and the air pollution in Caracas. Each of these smells brings back special memories and triggers all the emotions associated with each one.

Listening to God through the smells of nature is an obvious way to listen through our sense of smell.

Paul compares his visit from Epaphroditus and the gifts sent by the Philippians to a fragrant offering, like the sacrifices the Israelites made to God (Phil. 4:18, ESV).

18 I have received full payment, and more. I am well supplied, having received from Epaphroditus the gifts you sent, a fragrant offering, a sacrifice acceptable and pleasing to God.

What do we offer to the Lord that is like a fragrant offering before Him?

How are His words like a fragrant offering to you?

One of the most powerful stories in which we hear God's answer, evidenced by the sense of smell, is found in Daniel 3. I encourage you to read the entire chapter before I highlight a few specific portions of the story for our listening exercise today.

Any notes from Daniel 3?

After refusing to bow down to the golden statue, we see the response of the three Jewish servants of God in Daniel 3:16-18 (NIV).

16 Shadrach, Meshach and Abednego replied to him, "King Nebuchadnezzar, we do not need to defend ourselves before you in this matter. 17 If we are thrown into the blazing furnace, the God we serve is able to deliver us from it, and he will deliver us[c] from Your Majesty's hand. 18 But even if he does not, we want you to know, Your Majesty, that we will not serve your gods or worship the image of gold you have set up."

Wow! What faith! But this is not where our story ends, nor is it the focus of our listening today.

Daniel 3:26-27 (ESV)

26 Then Nebuchadnezzar came near to the door of the burning fiery furnace; he declared, "Shadrach, Meshach, and Abednego, servants of the Most High God, come out, and come here!" Then Shadrach, Meshach, and Abednego came out from the fire. 27 And the satraps, the prefects, the governors, and the king's counselors gathered together and saw that the fire had not had any power over the bodies of those men. The hair of their heads was not singed, their cloaks were not harmed, and no smell of fire had come upon them.

Campfires, fire pits, bonfires, even a barbeque grill... no matter how far away I sit from the actual flames of the fire or from the smoke, my clothes and my hair always smell of smoke after a few brief moments.

Yet for Shadrach, Meshach and Abednego, "No smell of fire had come upon them."

What was God's message for everyone that day, evidenced through the sense of smell? (Or as heard by Nebuchadnezzar, seen in his decree, Dan. 3:28-29?)

God's power is unrivaled. And His ability to save uncompromised, no matter what the circumstances. May that truth be a fragrant offering and encouraging reminder for you today.

Additional notes, thoughts, or drawings from listening through the sense of smell:

Week 6, Day 5
Touch and Hear His Goodness

Listening through touch is a bit more challenging for us to put into practice through these 40 days of devotion. However, I want to invite you to put on your thinking cap. Put on your listening ears. It is a physical act that mirrors our spiritual invitation.

We are commanded to love with heart, soul, mind and strength (Matt. 22:36-40). And this means listening with heart, soul, mind, and strength.

Run your finger over your ears, noticing the detail with which God made the unique folds and bends in the cartilage. No two ears are alike. And while the ears on the outside of our head help us filter the sound, that is not where the listening takes place.

The sound travels through the ear canal and vibrates the small bones and membrane, sending signals to our brain, which we interpret into speech and sound.

As our final listening exercise, through writing or drawing, we will use the sense of touch as a reminder that we have been "Called to Listen." We will renew our commitment to listen to our Master and our devotion to Him.

On the first ear (left):

Write or draw the things you have heard from God and reminders of how He speaks to you personally.

For the second ear (below):

In the curve of the ear, write out the phrase "Speak, for your servant is listening" (1 Sam. 3:10b). And add a piercing to the drawing, in representation of the passage in Exodus 21:5-6 (NIV) and our renewed devotion to the Master.

⁵"But if the servant declares, 'I love my master and my wife and children and do not want to go free,' ⁶then his master must take him before the judges. He shall take him to the door or the doorpost and pierce his ear with an awl. Then he will be his servant for life.

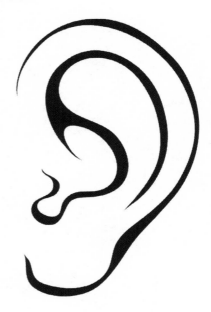

Week 6: **Listening through the five senses**

Each week, when we gather together, we will share the ways in which we have listened, what we have heard, and how we can continue to encourage and inspire one another in our listening. We have dedicated a time each day to listen to God and now we will devote some time listening to one another.

The following are the two questions we will ask and answer together each week.

1) What have you heard from listening through the five senses this week?

2) Which day's listening activity most resonated with you? And why that one?

Now, based on what we have each heard, we will share in the Common Threads (an Iron Rose Sister Ministries way of making any lesson, teaching, or reflection very personal and practical). The Common Threads help us focus in on the specifics of what we have heard and guide us into putting those things into practice, all in the context of community. They also serve as a form of spiritual journaling, which is why I encourage you to date them and look back later to see your growth.

Each woman's answers will be different because we hear unique things and each face different spiritual battles at any given moment. However, we can encourage one another to grow and bloom in those areas, remove thorns that hinder that growth, and hold each other accountable as iron sharpening iron.

Common Threads:

Date _____

An area in which you'd like to grow or bloom.

_____

_____

A thorn you'd like to remove.

_____

_____

An area in which you'd like to dig deeper or need someone to hold you accountable. (How can we, as a group, help you continue to listen or put into practice what you have heard?)

_____

_____

A message of hope, an encouraging word, or scripture from your time of listening.

_____

_____

Close each week in a time of prayer thanking God for what you have heard and bringing to God the requests shared through the Common Threads. This is an opportunity to join as one voice in our struggles, to rejoice in our victories, and to continue to listen to God and one another.

Conclusion

Love God. Love others. Listen to God. Listen to others.

For the past forty days of devotion, we have done exactly that. By developing our listening skills, we are better equipped to fulfill the greatest command (Matt. 22:34-39).

And since you have worked for forty days to create a new habit, don't stop now! You are well equipped to continue your devotion to listening to God and listening to one another.

For me, personally, my renewed commitment to listening can be summed up in the following two phrases, which I have repeated consistently over the past six weeks:

"Speak for your servant is listening."

"I'm listening to the still, small voice."

I still find it a struggle to listen. The noise of life invades my thoughts, even as I first awaken. C.S. Lewis[2] put it this way:

> The real problem of the Christian life comes where people do not usually look for it. It comes the very moment you wake up each morning. All your wishes and hopes for the day rush at you like wild animals. And the first job each morning consists simply in shoving them all back; **in listening to that other voice,** taking that other point of view, letting that other larger, stronger, quieter life come flowing in.

---

[2] Mere Christianity

And so on, all day. Standing back from all your natural fussings and frettings; coming in out of the wind.

We can only do it for moments at first. But from those moments the new sort of life will be spreading through our system: because now we are letting Him work at the right part of us. It is the difference between paint, which is merely laid on the surface, and a dye or stain which soaks right through.

My prayer for you specifically is that the things you have heard over the past forty days not be like a white-washed coating of paint. Rather, may what you have heard soak deep into your soul, transforming your heart, renewing your mind, and filling you with strength.

Love God. Love others. Listen to God. Listen to others.

Thanks for joining us on this listening journey. I can't wait to hear what God does in our lives from this point forward as we continue to listen!

Iron Rose Sister Ministries Bible Studies Format[3]

The Iron Rose Sister Ministries (IRSM) Bible Studies are designed for a small group context. Even if it were possible for me to give you "all the answers" and share my perspective on the verses and concepts being presented, I cannot emphasize enough the value of listening on your own, as well as the fellowship, discussion and prayer with other Christian sisters! The format of the IRSM Bible Studies allows for greater discussion, depth of insight and sharing of unique perspectives. If you don't follow the book exactly, that's ok! I invite you to make the studies your own, to allow the Spirit to lead, and to treat the studies as a guide and a resource, not a formula.

The IRSM Bible Studies also provide the opportunity for spiritual journaling on a personal level. I encourage you to date the chapters and add notes in the margins in addition to answering the questions. The 'Common Threads' will also allow you to chronicle

---

[3] This book is designed for personal study and *Weekly Reflections* in a small group context. While it is a slightly different format than the previous IRSM interactive Bible studies, the suggestions in a small group context are primarily the same.

your personal growth individually and in communion with your Iron Rose Sisters (part of the **Weekly Reflections**).

Using the image of the rose and the IRSM logo, the bloom of the rose represents areas we come to recognize in which we long to grow. Through these studies, we can also identify thorns we'd like to work on removing or need help to remove. They may be thorns like Paul's (2 Cor. 12:7-10), but by identifying them; we can know where they are and either dull them or stop sticking others and ourselves with them. The final Common Thread is the iron, which is best defined and facilitated in communion with other Christian sisters, Iron Rose Sisters.

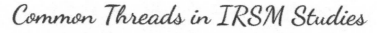

Common Threads in IRSM Studies

how you'd like to grow and bloom

a thorn you'd like to remove

an area in which you are striving to dig deeper or need to have someone hold you accountable

What is an Iron Rose Sister?

An Iron Rose Sister is a Christian sister who serves as iron sharpening iron (Prov. 27:17), encouraging and inspiring others to be as beautiful as a rose in spite of a few thorns.

Purposes of Iron Rose Sister Relationships:

➢ Encouragement and inspiration
➢ Prayer
➢ Understanding and affirmation
➢ Confidentiality
➢ Spiritual audit (IRS)
➢ Mutual call to holy living
➢ Spiritual friendship and conversation

Recommendations for Iron Rose Sister Ministries Bible Studies:

➢ Allow for an hour to an hour and a half meeting time weekly.
   o We're women—we like to talk!
   o Prayer time
   o Depth of conversation and discussion
➢ Rotate facilitating the weekly discussion among EACH of the women.
   o Everyone can lead!
   o Everyone will grow!
   o For additional suggestions, see the *Facilitator's Guide* (pg. 141-142)
➢ Commit to doing the **Daily Listening Exercises** ahead of time.
   o The discussion will be richer and deeper if everyone comes prepared, having listened.
   o How much you put in will be directly proportional to how much you get out.
   o You will need to do these studies with your favorite Bible in hand.
➢ Follow up with each other during the week.
   o Prayer

- o   Encouragement
- o   'Common Threads'

Facilitator's Guide

As presented in the *Iron Rose Sister Ministries Bible Studies Format*, the group is encouraged to rotate who leads the discussion each week.

Even if you do not feel equipped to lead or feel that you lack adequate experience to do so, it is a rich opportunity for growth and blessing. You are among sisters and friends that are supporting you in this part of your journey, as well.

Tips or reminders, especially for new leaders:

➢ Make it your own and allow the Spirit to lead—these studies are a resource, not a script.
  o Start with the first two questions on the *Weekly Reflections* page.
  o You are welcome to add questions of your own.
  o Highlight a *Listening Exercise* that most stood out to you, whether or not someone mentions it in the *Weekly Reflections*.
➢ Be willing to answer the designated discussion questions first, using your own examples, but avoid the temptation to do all the talking.

    o   Allow for awkward silence to provide the opportunity for others to share.

    o   It's okay to call on someone and encourage them to answer a specific question.

    o   "Why or why not?" or "Can you add to that comment?" are good follow-up questions for discussion.

➢ Leading is about facilitating the discussion, not about having all the answers.

    o   When someone brings up a difficult situation or challenging question, you can always open it up to the group for answers from Scripture, not just personal advice.

    o   The answer may merit further Bible study or the consultation of someone with more experience in the Word and/or experience regarding that type of situation. That's okay! We're digging deeper.

➢ The final question for discussion is the **Common Threads** in the **Weekly Reflections**. Thank those who are willing to share their authentic answers to these more vulnerable or personal questions that help us dig deeper and grow together.

➢ Be sure to budget some time for prayer.

➢ Remember our purposes as students of the Word and daughters of the King. We are striving listen and to deepen our relationships with God and one another—to be Iron Rose Sisters that serve as iron sharpening iron as we encourage and inspire one another to be as beautiful as a rose in spite of a few thorns.

About the Author

Michelle J. Goff has been writing small group Bible study materials in English and in Spanish throughout her ministry career. God has led Michelle to share these resources with more women across the world through Iron Rose Sister Ministries, a registered non-profit. She also continues to take advantage of opportunities for speaking engagements, seminars, women's retreats, and other women's ministry events across the Americas, in both English and in Spanish. If you would like to book a seminar in your area, please contact Michelle at ironrosesister@gmail.com, or for more information, visit www.IronRoseSister.com.

Personal Life

Michelle grew up in Baton Rouge, Louisiana, with her parents and three younger sisters. Her love and desire for helping women in their journey began early with her sisters, even when they thought she was being bossy. They've all grown a lot from those early years, but the sisterly bonds remain. Michelle has been blessed by the support of her family through all of her endeavors over the years.

Michelle enjoys time with family, cheering on the Atlanta Braves and the Louisiana State University Tigers, having coffee with friends, movies, travel, and speaking Spanish. And guess what her favorite flower is? Yep. The red rose.

She currently resides in Searcy, Arkansas, near her parents.

Ministry and Educational Experience

Michelle first felt called into ministry during her senior year at Harding University while obtaining a Bachelor of Arts degree in Communication Disorders and Spanish. She planned to join a team to plant a church in north Bogotá, Colombia, so she moved to Atlanta after graduating in May 1999 to facilitate that church-plant. Even though the plan for a Bogotá team fell through, Michelle continued her dream to be a part of a church plant there, which happened in March 2000.

She worked in the missions ministry at the North Atlanta Church of Christ for eighteen months before moving to Denver to work with English- and Spanish-speaking church plants there (Highlands Ranch Church of Christ and three Spanish-speaking congregations). During her two-and-a-half years there, Michelle continued her involvement in Bogotá and throughout various regions of Venezuela, visiting new church plants, teaching classes, conducting women's retreats, and speaking at and volunteering with youth camps.

In March 2003, Michelle moved to Caracas, Venezuela, to assist with a church planting on the eastern side of the city. Her time in Caracas was focused on the East Caracas congregation, but she was also able to participate in other women's activities across the country. In the four years Michelle spent in Caracas, the congregation grew from the twelve people meeting in her apartment to almost 100 meeting in a hotel conference room. The East Caracas congregation recently celebrated its twelfth anniversary and is still going strong in spite of the difficult economic and political situation in the country. A visit to Bogotá every three months to renew her Venezuelan visa also facilitated continued assistance with the congregation there.

In March 2007, Michelle transitioned back into ministry in the United States as the women's campus minister for the South Baton Rouge Church of Christ at the Christian Student Center (CSC) near the LSU campus. While walking with the college students on their spiritual journey and serving in other women's ministry roles, Michelle also pursued her "nerdy passion" of Spanish. She graduated from LSU in December 2011 with a Masters in Hispanic Studies, Linguistics Concentration. Her thesis explored the influence of social and religious factors in the interpretation of Scripture.

Michelle is now following God's calling to use her bilingual ministry experience with women of all ages and cultural backgrounds to bless them with opportunities for growth and deep spiritual connection with other Christian sisters through Iron Rose Sister Ministries.

About Iron Rose Sister Ministries

Vision:

To equip women to connect to God and one another more deeply.

www.IronRoseSister.com

Overall Mission:

A ministry that facilitates Christian sister relationships that will be like iron sharpening iron, encouraging and inspiring each other to be as beautiful as a rose in spite of a few thorns. Its goal is to provide women's Bible studies that are simple enough for anyone to lead and yet, deep enough for everyone to grow. These resources are available in English and Spanish (Iron Rose Sister Ministries - IRSM/Ministerio Hermana Rosa de Hierro - MHRH).

FACETS of Iron Rose Sister Ministries' vision:

F – Faithfulness – to God above all else. First and foremost: *"Seek first His kingdom and His righteousness and all these things will be added to you as well"* (Matt. 6:33).

A – Authenticity – We're not hypocrites, just human. *"But he said to me, "My grace is sufficient for you, for my power is made perfect in weakness." Therefore I will boast all the more gladly about my weaknesses, so that Christ's power may rest on me. That is why, for Christ's sake, I delight in weaknesses, in insults, in hardships, in persecutions, in difficulties. For when I am weak, then I am strong"* (2 Cor. 12:9-10).

C – Community – We were not created to have an isolated relationship with God. He has designed the church as a body with many parts (1 Cor. 12). The magnitude of "one another" passages in the New Testament affirms this design. As women, we have unique relational needs at various stages in life—whether we are going through a time in which we need, like Moses, our arms raised in support by others (Ex. 17:12) or are able to rejoice with those who rejoice and mourn with those who mourn (Rom. 12:15). The Iron Rose Sister Ministries studies are designed to be shared in community.

E – Encouragement through Prayer and Accountability – *"As iron sharpens iron, so one person sharpens another"* (Prov. 27:17). God has not left us alone in this journey. *"Confess your sins to each other and pray for each other so that you may be healed. The prayer of a righteous man is powerful and effective"* (James 5:16). It is our prayer that every woman that joins in this mission participates as an Iron Rose Sister with other women, partnering in prayer and loving accountability.

T – Testimony – We all have a "God story." By recognizing his living and active hand in our lives, we are blessed to share that message of hope with others (John 4:39-42). Thankfully, that story is not over! God continues to work in the transformation of lives, and we long to hear your story.

S – Study – *"The Word of God is alive and active. Sharper than any double-edged sword, it penetrates even to dividing soul and spirit, joints and marrow; it judges the thoughts and attitudes of the heart"* (Heb. 4:12).

In order to fully realize the blessing, benefit, and design of the Iron Rose Sister Ministries vision, we must go to the Creator. Through a greater knowledge of the Word, we can blossom as roses and remove a few thorns—discerning the leading of the Spirit, recognizing the voice of the Father, and following the example of the Son. This is more effectively accomplished in community (small group Bible studies), but not to the exclusion of time alone with God (personal Bible study).

For more information, please:

Visit www.IronRoseSister.com.

Sign up for the IRSM daily blog and monthly newsletter.

IRSM is a registered 501(c)(3) public nonprofit with a board of directors and advisory eldership.

Made in the USA
San Bernardino, CA
16 July 2017